Narrative of the Wreck of the Lady Munro, On the Desolate Island of Amsterdam, October, 1833 - Primary Source Edition

John McCosh

THE ISLAND OF AMSTERDAM.

NARRATIVE

OF THE

WRECK OF THE LADY MUNRO,

ON THE

DESOLATE ISLAND OF AMSTERDAM,

OCTOBER, MDCCCXXXIII.

BY J. M'COSH,
ASSISTANT SURGEON, HON. EAST INDIA COMPANY,
BENGAL SERVICE.

I'll read you matter deep and dangerous,
As full of peril and advent'rous spirit,
As to o'erwalk a torrent roaring loud,
On the unsteadfast footing of a spear.
SHAKSPEARE.

———— Quæque ipse miserrima vidi,
Et quorum pars magna fui.
VIRGIL.

GLASGOW:
PRINTED BY W. BENNET, FREE PRESS OFFICE.

1835.

NARRATIVE.

CHAPTER I.

On the 27th June, 1833, the barque Lady Munro, of Madras, burthen 250 tons, sailed from Calcutta towards Van Diemen's Land, *via* Madras and the Isle of France. The crew consisted of the captain, two European officers, and forty Lascars; amongst which last, the serang corresponded with boatswain, and the four tindels with boatswain's mates. The Lady Munro, after becoming crowded with passengers at Madras, and completing her cargo afterwards with sugar at Port Louis, sailed direct for Hobartown. On the 7th October, we had gone so far to the southward as latitude 36°, and, having got the steady westerly winds, we hoped for the completion of the voyage in one fortnight more.

We invalids were beginning to compliment one another on the improvement of our health and appearance, and congratulating ourselves on the enjoyment of such a delightful temperature, compared with the sultry, feverish atmosphere, from which we had so lately escaped. Our cloaks, and pea-jackets, and Guernseys, were now in full play, and amply repaying us in warmth and comfort for our provident care. The awning no longer shaded the quarter-deck, neither were we so lonely and destitute of objects of beauty and interest as a landsman would suppose, while floating like a solitary speck of cloud upon a whole hemisphere of azure blue. We could readily divest ourselves of the consciousness of being so many thousand miles distant from any habitable abode, by figuring to ourselves in the clouds, in one place, low-lying fertile shores, glowing in sunshine, and waving with yellow grain; in another, stupendous craggy mountains, dappled with mighty forests, and capped with snow; in a third, broad-spreading meadows, with the mist of a summer's evening settling upon them; and if, during the day, we were weary with gazing upon the ocean, in what few objects we chanced to meet with, we could frequently refresh our eyes on another sea, painted upon the evening sky of the most brilliant colours, varnished with the setting sun, and over-canopied with a sky of its own, of corresponding elegance and chasteness. There we could trace the progress of the little airy skiffs, gliding in an archipelago of enchanted islands—parting, mixing, and combining in the most miraculous manner—congregating into extensive continents, or evanishing into empty space. The long-tailed, snow-white tropic birds had forsaken us, and returned to their more congenial torrid zone. The timid flying-fish no longer skimmed the surface; the dolphin, with his bellows-pipe snout and horizontal tail, no longer played around our bows, and amused us with his gambols. Still we were not alone upon the waters: the Cape pigeon, with snow-white breast and painted wing, fluttered beneath the stern, picking up the crumbs that were thrown overboard. The stormy pettrils, more cautious, flitted like bees at a distance. The majestic albatross, the monarch of the seafowl race, soared along on wide-extended wing, from wave to wave, from cloud to cloud, and scanned our deck from stem to stern, with keen inquiring eye; while his rival of the finny tribe, emerged like a submarine vessel from the depths of the ocean, measured his length with ours, and, apparently satisfied with his superiority, spouted his antics contemptuously to the sky, and left us to follow in his wake.

The sun went down with more than usual splendour; the sky was clear and serene, with only one or two little clouds reposing upon it, like an auburn spot on the bosom of a beautiful female asleep. The wind seemed to have exhausted its strength during the day, and only a feeble breath flitted about, to convince us that it was only recruiting its energies. The ocean was, nevertheless, heaving its billows very high, and the well-defined circular margin of the liquid horizon, was frequently distorted by the lofty crest of some giant wave, that tossed up its foaming top to the sky. The starry train stepped forth from their concave of darkness, and shone upon the sea with their purest ethereal light; the moon, with all her inherent effulgence, was encircled with a halo of radiance, and fleeting meteors occasionally streamed along the sky, like angel messengers on some heavenly errand. Such a night could not fail to inspire us with the most pleasing emotions, and we sat assembled upon the poop till a late hour, singing the songs of our native land, and making party arrangements for the enjoyment of our time in Tasmania. Almost every passenger was more or less intimately connected with the country. Some expected to meet with a brother-in-law; some an affectionate sister; several a father and mother; and some with a wife and family,—and all were in the highest spirits at the thought of the near approaching happy meeting.

At noon, on the 11th October, our latitude was 37° 29′ S., longitude 75° 40′ E., making our direct distance from the islands of Amsterdam and St. Paul's about 110 miles. These two lonely islands formed the chief part of the evening conversation. The crowds of children on board, overcome with the noise, and restlessness, and mutiny of the day, lay fast asleep, and allowed us our limited portion of peace and quietness, as we sat all happy, assembled round the cuddy table, enjoying our tumbler of hot whisky-toddy. Some regretted that they could not have an opportunity of seeing them by daylight, and transmitting them to their portfolio;—some that they could not have a ramble and a pic-nic on shore, and a draught of the mineral springs;—some that they could not prove the possibility of catching fish in one pool of water, and throwing them off the hook into another to boil. The captain regretted that he could not have the pleasure of presenting us with a dish of fresh fish to breakfast; others, tired of the length of the passage, and anxious to get to their long-wished-for homes, rejoiced that the darkness of the night should prevent all delay; and several bets were laid that we should pass them by without seeing them at all. Thus the evening passed away in the usual pleasant manner; and we retired to our cabins all on the most cordial terms, resolved to be on deck next morning by sunrise, and probably to see the mountains astern; for the captain resolved to pass about thirteen miles to the northward of the northern island of the two, and expected to be up with it about two in the morning.

About half-past twelve, one of the passengers sent a servant to awaken me, and tell me (in joke, as I afterwards learned,) that land was in sight. I went on deck, and asked the serang, (the boatswain,—a native of India,) who was then keeping watch, if he saw land. But his answer was: "Na, saheb, likher hum alkhta,"—(No, sir, but we are looking out for it.) It was then a cold, dark, foggy night, with drizzling rain, and a stiff breeze, and the ship was dashing along, nine knots an hour, with all sail set, and the wind on the quarter. No moonlight shone upon the waters, no starlight glistened upon the sky; a dense cloud of mist enveloped us, and nothing but the snow-white crest of the following wave, and the phosphoric balls of light that rolled upon the galaxy of luminous animalculæ in our wake, lighted our path through the deep.

Not much relishing the joke played upon me, I went below, and turned into my cot, thankful that I could make myself so snug and comfortable, while so many poor fellows on deck, unused to such a cold temperature, stood shivering, drenched with rain, thinly and poorly clothed against such inclement weather. The lamp swung briskly in the cuddy, (the cuddy was between decks,) but no one kept watch by its glow; the wind sounded hollow in the sails, and whistled shrilly through the shrouds, and the rain-drops rattled upon the skylight; the tiller chains creaked upon their iron pulleys; the cabin doors jolted upon their hinges; and the water rippled swiftly along the sides, accompanied by the effervescing hiss of the foam-bells bursting: but no one was disturbed. Every one was fast asleep, and nothing but the long-drawn sigh, and the indistinct murmur of a dream, gave evidence of their existence.

I had not fallen asleep, indeed I had not turned in a quarter of an hour, when I heard a sudden, alarming voice, from the forecastle. It was instantly answered from the poop; a confused sound hurried along the deck; all the watch seemed in motion. Immediately after, the ship struck, and with such violence as almost to pitch me out of my cot. An awful pause ensued, as if the ship was stunned with the concussion, and incapable of motion. A few seconds after, she struck a second time, and with increased violence, till every plank in her frame trembled, and every iron bolt rang aloud. I heard the sea roaring and gurgling around my port, and dashing over the deck. I rushed up the companion ladder, with nothing on but my shirt and trousers. The water was dashing down it in cascades; the serang was running about, calling, "Captain Sahib! Captain Sahib! Johaz lagga! kya currenga! Hum kya currenga!" and crying like a child—(Captain! Captain! the ship has struck! What shall I do! What shall I do!)

After running from one hold to another, I succeeded in gaining the poop, and, to my horror, saw the bold, black, well-defined shore, within forty or fifty yards of the ship, with a tremendous surge dashing upon the rocks.

The ship now lay with her side to the sea, with her deck sometimes inclined to one side, sometimes to another; the waves tumbled in immense volumes over her, sweeping every thing fore and aft to destruction, and pouring down the hatchways in torrents. I thought my time in this world was now at an end, and looked upon every coming wave as my grave; and, as it passed over me, seemed to feel the coldness of death itself drawing nigh. My late wreck upon the Ganges appeared a piece of mimicry; the Chooar jungle, with all its mortality, a place of paradise; and oh! how gladly would I have taken the chance of another hopeless recovery from a six weeks' attack of jungle fever, rather than the risk of getting safe to shore. Why did I not die in a cultivated and a Christian land, where, soothed with the sympathy and affectionate kindness of my brother officers, when life burnt dimly in the socket—when existence was become a burden and a misery scarcely to be supported—when my transition to another world would have been comparatively easy, and where I could have laid my body to moulder into dust in a quiet grave!

Why was this warm tenement already restored to almost original energy, reserved to prove the feebleness of mortal efforts in the war of elements; to dash about on every surge, from wave to rock, and from rock to wave, a buoyant and a bloated corse; to be lacerated and broken upon the stones, mangled and mutilated by the monsters of the deep, torn into fragments like the wreck itself, and strewed along the desolate and savage shores, to macerate and whiten in the tempest; to become the sport of seals and seafowl, the wonder of some future castaway, the dateless record of some long-lost, never-heard-of vessel.

Such thoughts as these passed in rapid succession through my mind, till death, at this time, seemed too dreadfully awful to be encountered. Firmly resolved to struggle to the last, I collected all my senses, roused up every energy, selected the most secure position I could find, and, holding hard my breath as one surge after another rolled over me, making my very arms crack, I clung to the brass staunchions of the poop railing, with the convulsive grasp of a drowning man.

All the lights in the cuddy below were extinguished, and the night was so dark that one person could not recognise another. The ship staggered about from rock to rock, groaning and labouring, writhing from side to side, like a dying thing in its last agony; the sails and rigging were torn to tatters; the masts and yards went crashing overboard piecemeal, one after another, and fell seaward. Cries and shrieks of despair were now heard in the cuddy,—and the mother's cry of "Save my children! oh, save my children!" pierced me to the very soul. The united roar of the surf, the wind, and the crash of falling masts and spars, drowned every human cry; and the hull, at one time heaved high into the air, at another dashed with destructive force upon the rocks, gave one last lurch, and went all to ten thousand shivers. I was torn from my hold upon the poop, without knowing how, and amongst the dreadful breakers before I was aware of it, and swam strongly for the shore, amidst floating wreck, and groups of drowning men. I felt the fatal grasp of desperate hands pass two or three times around my thigh, when the first surf buried me, and once or twice felt my foot strike against some one struggling beneath me. I thought the hand of death itself was closing, and made the utmost possible exertions to get away. Sometimes I got entangled amongst pieces of the sails and rigging, but less dreaded their folds and coils; and frequently was struck by planks, and spars, and floating boxes. The first wave hurled me along in its crest with the velocity of a whirlwind, and I thought I would never again ascend to the surface; the second followed with equal impetuosity, and hurled me upon the rocks. I grasped a pointed projecting rock with both arms, till it receded; and, after a moment of distressing anxiety, lest a third should overtake me and sweep me away, I was high and dry, and my danger was over. I crawled along on hands and feet from rock to rock, till I came to a bank of reeds; and, thinking myself beyond reach of the surf, I gathered as many of them together as I could, and tying them into a knot, sat down under their shelter. By this time all the cries of the drowning had ceased, and nothing was heard but the rending of the wreck, and the thunder of the devouring elements. Indeed, the destruction of the ship was so awfully rapid, that most of the passengers must have been drowned in their cots, or before they had time to get out of their cabins. The captain and the chief mate were the only Europeans I heard on deck. Poor Aiken was utterly confounded; he cried out to the crew to cut away the topsail-haulyards, but no one ventured to do so, and the topsails went to pieces of their own accord; he ordered them to lower away the cutter, but the cutter broke her iron davits at the first or second bump, and was stove to pieces. The rudder was unshipped immediately after the ship struck; the stern was stove in; and the sea swept the poop cabin fore and aft. Seeing no hopes of the ship surviving many seconds, his whole attention was devoted to his wife and child. He was standing at the foot of the poop ladder, calling on Mrs. Aiken to come to him, and about to hand his child up to me on the poop, when the vessel went to pieces, and I saw him no more. His last words were, "Come here, Mary! Mary, come here!"

After repeated shouts to discover any other person who might have gained the shore, I was answered by one close to the water's margin. He continued to moan in the greatest distress, and, guided by his cries, I soon came to the place where he was. He did not know me; he had almost lost his reason, and took me for some person belonging to the island. He told me he was a poor unfortunate that had been shipwrecked in the Lady Munro, and that all his comrades had perished. He entreated me to have mercy upon him—to take him to a house and a fire, and give him a glass of grog, for he was perishing of cold; could not move a hand or a limb if it were to save his life, and was convinced he never could survive the injuries he had received. He was really in a very helpless condition; he was all over lacerated and bruised, and clotted with blood, and one of his arms was broken above the elbow. He was a stout, heavy man, and

I was unable to carry him on my back; but, after a good many efforts, I lifted him from stone to stone, till I got him out of danger from the waves, and seated him in the lee of a projecting rock. He continued to entreat me to take him to a fire, and give him a glass of grog; nor could I convince him that I was as helpless as himself. He then went on to give me a long account of the shipwreck—of the great number of people on board—and of their being all drowned but himself; when I could stand it no longer, and was forced to leave him. His name was Boyer, a soldier, and a convict from Bengal.

After returning to my knot of reeds, I cried at intervals, as loud as I could, to discover whether any other unfortunate was near; but no human sound was uttered in reply: the wild shore alone returned my call. Again and again did I eagerly look around me for some faint streaks of morning, to see whether we two, out of all the crowd, were saved; but hour after hour of darkness passed away, and no morning dawned. The rain poured down upon my bare head in torrents, and flowed in streamlets around my feet. Birds screamed in all directions amongst the rocks, alarmed at my intrusion. Some, more curious than the rest, alighted on my knot of reeds, and others, more sympathising, ventured to sit down on the stones beside me, and only left me when my teeth chattered with the cold, or when I beat my body with my hands, to keep up some degree of vital warmth. But I heartily disliked their confidence; for it only riveted the conviction, that I was cast away far from the abodes of man, upon a desolate and uninhabited island.

Never did the wheels of time seem so laden with delay; never was its progress marked by less defined periods. Not a star was in view, to tell, by its setting, the lapse of another half hour; not even the visible image of a cloud traversed the murky hemisphere. I counted the number of surfs, as they beat their concussions on the rocks at my feet, but found them somewhat irregular. I numbered the pulsations at my wrist, and found them also out of their wonted regularity. To pass away the time, I flung stones amongst the rocks, to silence or frighten the doubtful authors of such an unaccountable noise, and now and then caught a bird as it pryingly fluttered over my head, and had my fingers well bit and scratched for my pains. At length the combined noise beneath the rocks became louder and more deafening than ever, but soon after ceased, and the air became literally alive with birds. An ashy tint was painted upon the hem of the sky; the horizon became defined; a heavy mass of cloud slumbered here and there, along the liquid arch; a tinging with the faintest crimson—and the long-wished-for daylight appeared. Never did the radiance of heaven impart more welcome to my eye, or disclose such a melancholy scene.

There lay our late gallant vessel, in which I had spent so many days of happiness, piled upon the rocks, one shapeless mass of planks. I stood all alone amongst the reefs, gazing around me, but saw no living human being. I looked out upon the sea, and saw several of my fellow-passengers floating naked and lifeless upon the summit of the bursting wave. I raised my eyes to the dark frowning cliffs that overshadowed me, and saw nothing but the screaming seafowl. I looked upon my hands and feet, and found them bruised and bleeding; and yet I felt no pain. I tried to account for all these strange sights, but got bewildered in a perplexing maze. I began to distrust the evidence of my own senses—to think it all a delusion, the effects of some spell of enchantment, and was endeavouring to rouse myself to a state of consciousness and recollection, when I was convinced of its forlorn reality by the barking of two of the ship's dogs, which sprung from a crevice of a rock, and assailed me as if they had never seen me before. As soon as I spoke they recognised me, and, running up and fawning piteously, seemed to ask forgivenness for such an ill-timed attack. Roused by their noise, first one man, and then another and another, rose from amongst the rocks in different directions, till we mustered twenty-two; namely—The chief mate (Mr. Evatt) and myself, two European convicts, four native servants, and fourteen lascars. Every one was bruised and lacerated—several very severely.

The following list shows the number drowned:—

Capt. Aiken and brother, (second officer,)	2
Mrs. Aiken and child,	2
Mrs. Mountford and Miss Hazlewood of Madras,	2
Mrs. Capt. Brown and four children, (H. M. 57th Regiment,)	5
Captain and Mrs. Lardner, and three children, (50th Madras Native Infantry,)	5
Captain and Mrs. Knox, (6th Madras Cavalry,)	2
Lieut. and Mrs. Farmer, and one child, (H. M. 39th Regiment,)	3
Lieut. Clarke and two boys, (H. M. 62d Regiment,)	3
Quartermaster Lloyd, (H. M. 39th Regiment,)	1
Mr. Lawrie of Calcutta,	1
Mr. Monteath of Madras,	1
Mr. Fisher of Sydney,	1
Eight European Convicts, and four European Servants,	12
Nine native Servants, and twenty-six Lascars,	35
Total,	75

The serang was one of the crew saved. I asked him how he could possibly run the ship on shore, when land was so conspicuous: He answered, that he did see land, but, thinking it only a squally cloud, was ordering sail to be taken in, when she struck. We were then standing E. by S. by compass, or, allowing for variation, E. ½ N. The least alteration in our course, even 10 degrees more northerly, would have taken us clear of the island; and the wind was so advantageous at the time, that the vessel might have been luffed out and saved, when within 100 yards of the rocks.

Had we, during the darkness of the night, been run down at sea by some stronger power—had we split upon some newly-formed rock, or reef of coral never seen before; or, by a stress of weather, or some other accident, been unavoidably driven upon a well-known shore, and suffered all the waste of life it was our hard fate to suffer, the catastrophe would have admitted of some palliation, and been comparatively endurable;—but to run with the utmost possible precipitation, right before a strong breeze, and direct upon the lee shore of a bold, mountainous island, which we knew we were approaching, and which we were aware bordered upon our course at the farthest; to see the cliffs frowning over the mast-head, like an angry demon, warning the thoughtless pilot to keep away; to be within hearing of the awful surf thundering upon the rocks, and to dash into the midst of the destructive breakers, till the dying groan of the ship gave warning of the approaching calamity,—this, this was the woful grievance; and yet the apathetic author of all our misfortunes—the shivering aboriginal of a tropical clime—outlived the horrors of the scene, and the sacrifice of 75 human beings committed to his unworthy care. Yet, withal, we have reason to be thankful, for we must have passed within a few feet of a low rock, about two hundred yards out at sea, on which, had we struck, every soul must have perished; or, had we gone on shore on one of the many bold headlands, instead of a shelving reef, no one could have survived to tell the mournful tale. On inquiring at the different survivors, I learned that many of the lascars fled to the rigging, in the hopes of being washed ashore upon the masts; but, as they all fell towards the sea, not one of them escaped. Three lascars were saved by cutting away the jolly-boat; the greater number held on by the poop deck till it was cast ashore, and had little more trouble than walking off it on to the rock. Two, like myself, escaped by swimming through the surf; one or two found themselves safe without knowing how; and one of the convicts maintains he made ashore astride upon the stock of the bower anchor. This may be accounted for by supposing that the anchor floated ashore upon the forecastle deck, to which it was lashed. Not one of the convicts was encumbered by irons, or under any restraint at the time; they were all stout, active, able-bodied men.

After muster, we wandered along the shore, examining every creek and crevice, trying to find out some poor fellow who might have survived the waves of the preceding night, and not have strength to walk, but were not fortunate in finding one,—no, not even the last remains of one. Many pieces of the wreck still floated amidst the breakers, and now and then a head or limb rose to the surface and disappeared. The shore, for miles together, was strewed with planks, and spars, and fragments of casks and boxes; shreds of canvass, and empty sugar bags, and clothes of all descriptions. Every piece of cloth was torn to rags, fretted, and cut to pieces by the stones, or rolled round and between them, so as to be for the most part inextricable. The stoutest packages were stove asunder; the thickest bolts bent like so much lead; the corners of the beams ground off, and worn almost round. I observed a gun-case on shore, which I had often seen on board,—a very stout mahogany case, strongly clasped with brass, and buckled into a thick leathern case; yet, when I saw it, the case was a mass of splinters, and nothing of the gun remained in the bag but the stock.

Every one covered himself with what clothes he could find, as they lay dripping upon the stones. My dress, when completed, consisted of the shirt and trousers in which I came ashore; a red jacket, with one of the sleeves torn off; a flannel shirt over all, tied round the waist with a silk handkerchief; a silk scarf for a turban; a shawl round my neck; and a leopard's skin over my shoulders. The lascars were a great deal more extravagant, and were contented with nothing less than straw-bonnets, and turbans of Cashmere shawls and China crape; hanging upon their bodies the ladies' richest dresses, and pieces of splendid uniform; hiding their *horny* hands and feet in kid gloves and silk stockings; and literally loading themselves with webs of silks, and muslins, and flannels, till they could carry no more. The most interesting objects that we met with were several entire bags of rice and while Mr. Evatt and myself were engaged in rolling them out of reach of the sea, and providing against immediate starvation, these thoughtless people were strolling about, breaking open packages, and secreting their contents; nor could we convince them of their destitute condition, nor obtain their assistance to secure food for themselves to eat, and which another tide might sweep away. Towards evening we returned to the scene of desolation, carrying with us a dead sheep and a piece of salt beef that we found, and attempted to kindle a fire. Most providentially, a small box of chemical matches was cast on shore, and also a number of wax candles. By dipping a match into the small bottle, we easily kindled a flame, but found it not so easy to communicate it to the wet wick. After consuming about a dozen matches to no purpose, the idea suggested itself of breaking a candle into two, and getting a dry piece. This we did, and soon kindled the candle; but our difficulty was only half over. We could not set fire to the wood, still saturated with water; it was in vain that we cut it into slices, and mixed it with pieces of wax, and piled it in a cask, to shelter the flickering and feeble flame till it should kindle. After an hour spent in fruitless attempts, our eye happened to fall upon an old cocoa nut, which we had picked up and intended to eat; we cut it open, tore the fine dry husk to pieces, and, mixing it with the wood and wax, soon kindled our fire, and broiled a piece of the sheep, and roasted a piece of yam and an onion, for supper, or rather for breakfast, for it was our first meal. It still continued to rain heavily, and we had provided no kind of shelter for the night; we were as wet as water could make us, and perishing of cold. Something was to be done. Several large casks lay upon the beach; we got two of them rolled above high water-mark, and pouring out the water they contained, placing the two open ends in opposition, Mr. E. and I crept in, drew them together, and covered up the space between them with a cloth. For some time we congratulated ourselves on our new abode, and thought if we could not lie down dry, we could at least prevent ourselves from becoming wetter, and could keep up a tolerable degree of steaming heat. But before midnight we were convinced of our mistake; for the coldness of the cask condensing our breath, we were almost floating, and, indeed, might have done so, if the water had not found its way out by the bung. We lay shivering all night; the cramp tortured us in every limb; we could not sit upright; we had not room to turn ourselves; and, therefore, spent one of the most horribly uncomfortable nights possible. When we emerged into open air this morning, (13th October,) we were steaming like a boiler, and could hardly stand erect. The lascars were looking most miserably, and saying such another night of rain and cold would kill them all. We found the convict who had been so dreadfully injured, cold and lifeless; and were informed that the other convict had last night found a bottle of brandy, and put it into his hands to take a mouthful; but he drank it to the bottom before taking it from his head, and never spoke after. Our first object was to get the body removed to a distance, for we intended building a house on the same spot. Bury it we could not, for there was not an ounce of soil or sand to be seen; to burn it was against our nature; and to leave it before our eyes, and on our every-day path, was what we could not think of doing; so, with the assistance of the remaining convict, and one of the cuddy servants, we took each an extremity, and, lifting it from rock to rock, got it removed to the water's edge, and there left it to be swept away by the next tide.

There being no appearance of the rain ceasing, we obtained the assistance of three lascars, to carry over the fly of a tent that we saw the day before. About noon, we got it brought to the most convenient spot we could find, and pitched it, making the ropes fast to the stones. The walls we completed by pieces of rock, and the floor we brought somewhat near a level by planks and gratings; thus erecting a very tolerable habitation. The lascars had also got themselves under cover, and were all clubbed together, as their different castes and countries admit of. They were a most heterogeneous pack,—consisting of Africans, Arabs, Hindoos, Birmese, Malays, Manillamen, and Portuguese. These were again subdivided by petty quarrels amongst themselves. Several of them were desperate characters; some of them lived under cover of a projecting rock; some under a shade, formed by a few spars laid against a perpendicular rock, and covered with cloth; some in the crevice of a rock, sheltered with a kind of awning; and others, rather than separate from the main body, erected a kind of roof; while one or two individuals, more apathetic than the rest, crammed themselves into clothes-baskets and empty boxes. A large box made a very good house, especially where extension, as with the natives, is a matter of indifference; and, by laying it on one of its sides, it affords, if necessary, the advantage of a verandah.

CHAPTER II.

Having thus procured for ourselves a small supply of food, and being provided with such accommodation as circumstances permitted, we were more at liberty to explore our situation. Next to our own preservation, upon a perilous and unsheltered rock, our first care was to search for the bodies of those of our fellow-voyagers, with whom we had so lately held delightful converse. In our search we found a great many bodies on shore, and recognised most of them. The scene was mournful and melancholy beyond description: here lay the helpless infant, that had just begun to lisp the name of mother, far away from its mother's protecting and affectionate arms, cradled upon the naked rock; there the lively, romping girl, all silent and still, who never knew silence or stillness before: here the promising, hardy boy, with features distorted by fear, who before was a stranger to what fear was; there the tender mother of the babe unborn, with her raven tresses dishevelled and wound around her arm, so provident of late for the coming of her little stranger: here the doting husband, lately so full of vigour, stretched along the cold stones, like a tree in its green leaves rooted up by a flood; there the venerable soldier at rest after all his toils, and hairbreadth 'scapes from war and pestilence, when about to retire upon the fruits of a life of service: here the young man entering upon the campaigns of life, high in hope, elated with favourable anticipations of the future, and eager to commence his career; there the emaciated, melancholy invalid, freed the thousand real "ills that flesh is heir to," and the tens of thousands of imaginary sorrows, who, for years together, wore the insignia of the tomb, and every evening said, "To-morrow! ay, to-morrow! shall I enter into my rest," and my troubles shall be over: here the man of the world, whose life had been devoted to the amassing of an honourable independence, separated from his well-earned fortune, when hastening home to enjoy it in the land of his boyhood, with all the fascinating hallucinations of earthly happiness; there our much-esteemed little captain, the tender husband, the affectionate father, and the dutiful son—the proven friend, the ornament of his profession, and the favourite of us all—through whose veins circled the warmest milk of human kindness, and on whom the widowed and the destitute so often bestowed their grateful benedictions: here the sable crew, congregated from all the points of the compass, amphibious in their habits, and at home amongst the breakers, like wreaths of sea-weed washed on shore!

Alas! no hallowed turf pillowed their heads; no chaplet of roses spread their perfumes around their graves; no "storied urn nor animated bust" recorded their untimely end! The midnight rush of the waters awakened them but to take farewell of this world; their parting breath was committed to the waves; the whelming sea rolled over them like a shroud, and lulled them to their long and last repose! No insulting visitant shall disturb their shell-studded bed; no unhallowed footstep shall pollute their rocky home! The lichens of the rocks shall embroider their pall; the tangled sea-weed shall wreath its fillets and festoons around them, and the dew of the evening shall embalm them with its tears; the sea-birds wild shall sing their sweetest anthems; the melancholy penguin shall sentinel their pillow, and the glow-worms of the deep shall trim their midnight lamps through the silence of the night; the gloom of the o'erhanging cliffs, and the mists of the lava mountains shall hang their mournful drapery over them, and the starry vault of the sky shall o'ercanopy their last earthless abode!

He who has strayed along the lately over-flown banks of some upland river, and marked with careful eye the opening bud, the full-blown flower, the aromatic shrub, and the leafy towering tree, swept away from their native soil, denuded of all their foliage, lacerated in their branches, strewed singly along the stony bank, or congregated into promiscuous groups, behind some flood-resisting rock,—he only can form an adequate conception of the prostration of human life. Some of these may again take root, and bud, and flourish, and delight the eye as before; but no spring shall reanimate the remains of the drowned, for corruption and decay have already impressed their livid seal upon their bosom!

When I reflected that these cold and motionless bodies,—still fresh with life, with the hue of the rose still upon their cheek, but for too great a degree of patient endurance under so many bodily injuries, too much composure and resignation to such a flinty and comfortless bed, and something constrained and unnatural in the disposure of their limbs, apparently only asleep,—were but two days ago warm with life, high in hope, and busily employed in projecting plans for future enjoyment, active and valued members of society, and holding such high places in the estimation of all who knew them,—the past appeared to me as a dream, and I turned away from the affecting scene, indulging in the idea!

How true to nature did these very expressive lines of Byron then appear!—

"He who hath bent him o'er the dead,
Ere the first day of death has fled,
Before decay's effacing fingers
Have swept the lines where beauty lingers,
And marked the mild angelic air,
The rapture of repose that's there,—

The fixed yet tender traits that streak
The languor of the placid cheek;
And but for that sad, shrouded eye,
That fires not, wins not, weeps not now,
And, but for that chill, changeless brow;—
Yes! but for these, and these alone,
Some moments, ay, one treacherous hour,
We still might doubt the tyrant's power.
So fair, so calm, so softly sealed,
The first, last look, by death revealed;
So coldly sweet, so deadly fair,—
We start, for soul is wanting there;
Their's is the loveliness in death,
Which parts not quite with parting breath
But beauty with that fearful bloom,
That hue which haunts it to the tomb.
Expression's last receding ray,
The farewell beam of feeling past away;
Spark of that flame, perchance of heavenly birth,
Which gleams, but warms no more its cherished earth."

On the 14th, I slept a little more comfortably, with two trunks for my bed, a tiger skin for my mattress, my wet clothes, and a blanket still wetter, for my covering. In making preparations for breakfast, I found the sheep picked to the bone, and the piece of salt beef gone; a lazy scoundrel, a son of Mahommed, engaged in cutting a large gap out of our only ham. However, I saved him the trouble of carrying it away, and broiled a portion of it, with some rice and pumpkin, and drank a bottle of soda water, for breakfast.

During the day, we ascended a range of high mountains, overlooking the scene of our suffering, and planted a white flag on the highest point, making use of a bamboo, tied upon an oar, for a staff, and a sheet for the flag. We found the ascent very steep and rugged, and the rocks loose and easily detached, so that we had much difficulty in getting the oar passed along from one to another. We penetrated about a mile into the interior, till we discovered another higher range of mountains, when we retreated, not seeing a shrub on our journey; indeed, nothing but bare rocks, and a jungle of reeds, higher than our heads, so dense as to be almost impassable. We saw no traces of the existence of man, no quadrupeds of any kind, and no water. We caught three birds amongst the rocks, which proved valuable pickings, and we found a nest with two eggs, which we carried off, to the great distress of the owners. On our return, we dressed them with a hotch-potch of rice, wheat, ghee, pumpkins, yams, onions, and a kind of wild parsley, which we found amongst the rocks. We were but poorly supplied with cooking utensils; all we could muster being a set of curry dishes, a tea-pot, a pewter basin, and two or three pieces of a tin box; and these again stood substitutes for dish and platter. The luxury of a table or chair we never thought of; a good teak plank, the broadest on the floor, answered all useful purposes; our fingers, *a la Mussulman*, performed the part of fork and spoon, and a soda water bottle that of a drinking cup.

This was the first dry day since we were cast away, which enabled us to dry our clothes, and added very much to our comfort. The afternoon we spent in making more platforms for drying rice; decanting water out of casks, still exposed to the surf, into others above danger; sewing canvass soles upon my only pair of socks; repairing the tear and wear of my pantaloons; and adding a couple of pockets to my jacket. My hands and feet were in a miserable state with sores and bruises.

We now began to reflect seriously upon our situation, and, in spite of our constant and active employment, our forlorn prospects threw at times a dark cloud over the future. We were then twenty-one in number, cast away upon a desert island, with nothing to subsist on but a limited supply of damaged rice; without the probability of a wild beast to prey upon, or a shell-fish larger than a finger nail, when our scanty stock of provisions should be exhausted. We were walled in by a mountainous surf, the very noise of which continued to strike upon our ear with terror,—thousands of miles distant from any human habitation, and so much the dread of the mariner, that few ventured nearer its shores than merely to see it dim on the horizon, and be convinced of its existence. The lascars were also gloomy and despondent, seldom moving out of their huts, or sitting dumb and motionless upon the rocks for hours together, staring on vacancy. When asked what they thought of their situation, they answered, with stoic and provoking indifference, "Sub chan moorjaga." (We will all die here.) I was much struck with the expression of Abu-bukhir, an Arab, the best man amongst the whole. On my asking why he was so downcast and melancholy, his reply was, "Hum na dirta Sahib, likhen hum log ekhus hae! Kya curriga!!" (I am not afraid, Sir; but we are twenty-one in number. What shall we do?)

The 15th was another busy day amongst the grain and water. We had then secured about fourteen bags of rice, one of wheat, a few yams, pumpkins, and onions, a bacon ham, some ghee, and eight bottles of wines and liquors, with a dozen bottles of soda water; and from these we had to select our bill of fare. It seemed impossible that when planks and masts were dashed to pieces, such a frail article as a bare bottle could escape; yet almost all the bottles we saved were lying upon the naked rocks.

We breakfasted that morning upon a piece of a pumpkin that lay on the beach; having first rooted out a thriving colony of shell-fish that inhabited the pulp. We thought of eating fish and all together but such was rather incompatible. To my great joy, I saw a penguin standing amongst the wreck; he was a stupid-looking bird, and allowed me to approach within a few yards of him, without being the least discomposed. I took up a stone and knocked him over, but it did not much injure him, for he ran for the water as fast as he could; but I outran him, and captured him after an obstinate resistance. He was a very singular bird, about two feet high, of a dark colour, and covered with something between fur and feather, partaking of the nature of both. He had a very fine top-knot of narrow yellow feathers, that flowed upon his neck, and his bill was like a crow's; his feet were webbed, and placed very far back, and his wings were out of all proportion—small, and quite useless for flying. He was very heavy to his size; fat, and promised to be good eating; but when cooked, as black and dry as a piece of turf; in fact, he was anything but palatable. Had it not been for his bill, he might have passed for a young seal.

CHAPTER III.

It was truly degrading to human nature to witness the apathy and indolence of the lascars, in providing for their own subsistence, or making any kind of exertion to hasten their departure from the island. All the provisions that were saved were collected by Mr. Evatt and myself, and two or three others, coaxed on at times to assist us. A great deal of the rice was spoiled from want of proper attention to drying it; for though it did not become bad so long as it lay in the water, yet if it had been allowed to remain in the bay one day, in the open air, or a few hours on the platform, unturned, it became heated and discoloured, and unfit for any thing. Even this afternoon, we could not get men enough to carry the rice when dried to the casks. They became almost mutinous; and when asked by the chief mate to do any thing, their answer was, "Tumhara barabar abi hae. Tumhara nokhar channa hoga." (I am as good as you are now. I shan't be your servant here.) Plunder was their only occupation. That we could have excused; but they took every opportunity of entering our tent, in our absence, and carrying off the few things we had saved from the surf, for our own use. We saw some one or another, every day, wearing articles of clothing that originally belonged to us; and when asked to restore them, they shewed such a spirit of mutiny and resistance that we judged it safest to let them alone; but we trusted to have an opportunity of claiming them, if ever we were fortunate enough to get on board another vessel. Even those whose duty it was to cook on board ship, could rarely be got to make a cake of rice and water for us, so that we preferred cooking in our own turn, to being troubled with them. The convict Forsyth was scarcely a shade better than they, and boarded along with them. He was transported from the Mauritius for attempting to murder one of the serjeants of the regiment. The day before, a quantity of ghee was washed on shore, which was divided on the spot, and a portion was sent to us, although several of them complained because we got any at all.

When we looked into their hovels amongst the rocks, there they lay, slothfully, upon bundles and webs of cloth, smoking tobacco, or dead drunk, and quarrelling. Every slave boiled his rice in a silver teapot, and drank his muddy water out of a crystal decanter,—lighted his lair up with a wax candle, and anointed his loathsome body with the most costly oils and perfumes.

To shew their infatuation: Two days before, a bag of leaf tobacco was found on shore,—every inch of it they dried, and preserved most carefully; and carried their ingenuity and industry so far as to patch up a hubble-bubble, out of a cocoa nut, a piece of bamboo, and the neck of a bottle. Those who could not get a piece at the hubble-bubble, made their tobacco into the form of a cigar; and when the remains would not admit of that shape, they made tubes of paper, and stuffing them with the crumbs, smoked them paper and all. Yet these same people, would not, of their own accord, have dried one bag of rice, although they knew they had nothing else to subsist on. What was to be the issue I was afraid to think. Any attempt to introduce a system of abstinence or economy, was hopeless. Would there had been only two more of ourselves to form the stronger party, or that we could have separated our interests from theirs, and left them to their knives, and their fates!

Often had we occasion to remark, how kindly provident it was that none of the ladies or children were reserved to share in our miseries; for they must inevitably have sunk under it. God knows our calamities were heavy enough; but what would they have been, to be accompanied by the cries of a child for bread and water, which we had not in our power to give; or the silent tears of an amiable and accomplished lady, pining away under the load of her bereavement, and sinking into a grave for want of the common necessaries of life!

On the evening of the 15th, we prepared a table cloth for a flag, and went off next morning along the shore, towards the S.W. point of the island, to plant it. We had walked about four miles, when we came to a bold, bluff headland, that prevented us from getting farther. There we ascended the highest rock we could, and erected our flag, along side of a large lump of lava, securing the staff with ropes made fast to bunches of rushes. A tremendous surf broke all along the shore, which rendered it impossible for any boat to land. The rock was very lofty, and quite perpendicular; composed of soft, spongy-looking lava, with veins of a closer and harder consistence. One place evidently was the remains of a volcanic crater; but there were no traces of any inhabitant, save the albatross and the sea-hen, soaring and screaming in mid air. To our unspeakable joy we discovered a small streamlet of water, rippling over the precipice, and falling like a shower; of which we drank heartily, at the expense of a wet jacket. We found fine spar upon the beach, with the grass growing over it; but saw none of our own wreck in this direction, except one solitary parcel of Mirzapore carpets. Before we got back to our tent the tide had set in, and we had to watch a favourable opportunity in rounding the rocks, lest the surf should have caught us. As it was, several of the party were overtaken by their old enemy, and soundly ducked.

We were still engaged on the 17th with our rice

and wheat, and had got two large casks, one at each side of the door, nearly full, a box of wheat inside, and a cask of water in front. Though we might have expected the tides to be falling every day with the wane of the moon, yet, from the prevalence of strong westerly winds, they were every day becoming higher. The pile of planks and spars was now swept all away, and scattered along the shore. The first flag we planted was that morning blown all to tatters, which obliged us to sit down and sew four handkerchiefs together, which we erected lower down the mountain.

The birds we caught were a great blessing to us; and strongly reminded us of the provision made for the Israelites in the wilderness. During the day, these birds went away to sea, and returned in the evening, flying about as numerous as white ants before a shower. The air was literally alive with them: they had not room enough to fly, were constantly running against one another, and knocking each other down. We had no more trouble in catching them than to sit down in the crevice of a rock, so as to escape being struck by them as they flew, and pick them up as they alighted to sleep amongst the stones. The cooing noise they there made was intense. Though we did not move out of our tent, we might catch as many as we wanted inside; and, indeed, I have frequently caught them while engaged in cooking some of their comrades, and could hardly keep them out of the frying-pan. These birds, though not the most delicious in the world, did very well for hungry people; for, though tedious and troublesome to prepare, they occupied a good part of the time which might otherwise have hung heavy upon our hands. The lascars cut their throats, and ate them by the dozen, till they became sick and surfeited, converting our hamlet into a regular Golgotha, and clothing the rocks with their feathers. They were about the size of a jackdaw, and in colour, shape, and note, a good deal resembled a pigeon; but they were webfooted, and bit very hard. We called them our chickens. We saw thousands of fish every day swimming out beyond the surf, but they were far beyond our reach. Sometimes we thought of making a catamaran, and going out to them, but the rocky shore was a sad discouragement. We had saved the long line and a bundle of hooks, and longed for an opportunity of trying our luck.

On the morning of the 18th, we intended to make an excursion towards the north-east side of the island, but the surf was beating too high against the bold rocks to allow us to pass along the beach. We had always entertained the hope of finding the remains of some sealer's hut upon that side, or some cave, which we might convert into a place of living. It was very evident that no boat could render us any assistance upon this side, although we might attract the notice of some vessel; and there were no chances of any ship touching at the island, except upon the other side. Another inducement for going to the other side, was the certainty of being able to take plenty of fish, where there was most likely no surf to prevent us.

The tide still continued to encroach upon our encampment, so as to induce us to think seriously of removing to higher ground. We had already selected a spot about thirty feet higher, and completed the floor of our intended dwelling; but this was no easy task, where there was not a yard of soil, nor a foot of level rock. The plan we adopted, was to support two parallel beams upon four points of rock, as near a level as we could find, and cover these with planks ranged at right angles. The interstices afforded free admission for light and air, and the space beneath answered the place of cellars. The intercourse had to be kept up from rock to rock by platforms and ladders. Most of us were suffering severely from diarrhœa, the consequence of every thing we ate being saturated with salt water, and decomposed. We spent the night in fear and trembling, lest the surf should break into our tent, and sweep us out. If our fear was groundless, not so was our trembling; for the sea made the very rocks beneath us tremble like the shock of an earthquake.

We got up before daylight on the 19th, and made preparations to decamp; but were too late to save half a cask of water from being swept away, together with several platforms of rice and wheat. We mustered all the hands we could to save the rice, and though every surge threatened to rob us of our whole stock, such was the apathy of the lascars, that we could muster no more than half a dozen. Before we got all things removed, the surf was dashing into our tent. How one-half of those saved from the wreck could have survived such a surf was to me inconceivable. It first broke about one hundred yards out at sea, and could not be less than twenty feet high. It then came foaming along in awful grandeur to the shore, threatening to wash the mountain tops, and sweep their lichens away. There was something fearfully interesting in the contemplation of such a surf—much of grandeur and sublimity; and often have I spent a pleasant hour, after the toils and tumbles of the day were over, sitting upon some high rock, scanning the horizon with sail-searching eye, watching the sun's last rays radiating amongst the eclipsing clouds, and poring with wonder on the irresistible surge that raged beneath. Nor were my solitary hours of twilight without their enjoyment: we had saved lots of wax candles, and could afford a cheerful light to dissipate the gloom. My blacklead pencils and paper then came into play, and I scribbled away the hours till bedtime, when a hard teak plank, with a tarry blanket, and a bundle of tatters for a pillow, sufficed for the comforts of the night. But the wings of Morpheus hovered not over my couch, nor were my slumbers of unbroken forgetfulness. The slightest sound, the fall of a stone, the tent-fly flapping with the wind, the flutter of some wandering bird, or the rustle of the reedy jungle, fell upon my distempered ear like a shock of alarm, and I awoke upon my feet. The roar of a surf, louder and mightier than the rest, required all, and sometimes more than all, the philosophy I could muster, to assure myself that hitherto it could not come. Phantom-shipwrecks, as distinct, as palpable, and as distressing as the sad reality, haunted my disturbed imagination. Frequently did I fancy myself pacing the quarter-deck, in conversation with my fellow-passengers, and awaken at the sound of my own voice, or by a fall amongst the stones; and not a night passed but I saw some one or other rising from his watery grave, wandering lonely amongst the cliffs, with distorted limbs and mutilated body, in wayward and imperturbable silence.

In my lonely stroll along the shore that afternoon, I paid more attention than usual to the pieces of wreck that lay upon the beach. In one place lay the top of the individual hencoop on which we were wont to sit assembled on an evening, and talked and sang the twilight away; in another, a green-painted board, that once formed part of the stern sheets of the cutter. These three letters, M U N, lately graced her stern, the short-lived labours of poor C. That shapeless mass of wood, still partly afloat, lately guided our course through the deep, and near it lay the remains of the wheel, with its brass clamps started, and three-fourths of the spokes broken. High heaved on that piece of rock, lies the frame of my own cabin door, with all its venetians carried away; there lies the lid of my writing-desk, with the brass plate rooted up; and near it lies the beam on which, for months together, my cot was hung. There lies the remnant of our gaily-gilded figure-head, disfigured and mutilated, with her alto-relievo features ground into shapeless rotundity, her bosom all chafed and lacerated by the rocks, and her golden tresses bereft of one-half of their profusion. That shapeless Leghorn once adorned the face of the gay and good-natured Mrs. A.; that silken slipper lately added grace to the fairy foot of the amiable Mrs. B.; and that auburn mantle, only two days ago, hung its flowing folds on the handsome person of our favourite Mrs. C. That bill of exchange was in favour of Captain ——; that parchment contains the commission of Lieutenant ——; that other conferred the honour of Grand Knight Templar on Lieutenant ——; and there is the lid of the snuff-box of Lieutenant ——, with the scene of Dumbarton Castle still undefaced. That tortoise-shell comb, that telescope, that ivory work-box lid, that pincushion, that puff-box, that pocket compass, that hair-brush, that empty watch-case, that pair of stays, that greatcoat, music-book, amber necklace; that cocked hat, trunk lid, ivory-handled, flower-fringed parasol; that packet of letters of introduction, that chess-board, razor-strop, mess account-book; that bouquet of artificial flowers, footstool, scent-bottle, card-case, and piano-forte frame, could all be traced to their original owners; but, alas! who was there amongst us, of whom some sad relic could not be picked up in remembrance!

Many pieces of the wreck still floated in the water. When the tide was low, we could sometimes see the ribs of the bottom of the ship, in the trough between the waves. Two of the largest anchors lay so near the shore as to be partly uncovered, and a large iron knee, with only a splinter of wood attached to one side, lay high and dry, and twisted almost out of shape. The masts, the yards, the bowsprit, lay about in as many fragments as if they had been made of clay, and thrown from the cliffs that overlooked them, upon the rocks below.

The 20th was employed in making preparations for our intended excursion, viz.—sewing together another flag, pounding rice, and baking it into cakes, parching wheat for coffee, roasting yams and onions, and grilling chickens. "O, what a falling off is there, my countrymen!" would have been the first expression of many a social fellow, on discovering me seated upon my hams, amongst a cluster of rocks, with my eyes shut, to save them from the ill-natured smoke that wrung the very tears out; blowing the faggots to blacken a lump of dough on a tin plate, which even our starving dogs disdained to eat, or stirring about a morsel of rice with a spike nail, burning black, though for no fault of mine, but for want of sufficient fresh water to boil it. But no! Somebody says—

"Warriors and kings were cooks, or history lies:
Patroclus broiled beef steaks to quell his hunger,
The mighty Agamemnon potted conger,

And Charles of Sweden, 'midst his guns and drums,
Spread his own bread and butter with his thumbs;"—

And why not I?

Strange as it may appear, salt water was nearly as difficult to be procured as fresh. If we waited till the surf dashed up to its height, we got nothing but a bucketful of froth; if we followed its backward course till it stopped, and then filled our bucket, we were sure to be overtaken with our load by the next surf, and the consequences might have been critical. The plan we used was to lay fast hold of a rock, as near as we could guess half way between the rise and fall, and with the certainty of getting wet all over, and the chance of having a stone or two hurled against our shins by the receding wave, there we filled our bucket and ran. There is an old proverb somewhere which says, "Send him to the *sea*, and he will not be able to find salt water." I doubt the sage author of the above would not much like to have his dexterity put to the test on the weather shore of Amsterdam.

During the night we experienced a thunder storm, accompanied by rain and hail showers. On the morning of the 21st, we intended going off for the N.E. side of the island; but Mr. E. was laid up with the diarrhoea. I went scrambling amongst the rocks in the morning, expecting to find some drops of rain-water in the hollows; but every little handful was quite brackish. Reduced to the last extremity, I picked up a pair of pantaloons, and, tying a knot upon each leg, stowed two bottles into each, threw them over my shoulder, and, buttoning the waistband in front, set out, with my barefeet and my bamboo, along the shore, in quest of the water we discovered several days before. But the tide was beating so high against the rocks, that I had not advanced a mile when I was obliged to retreat. However, on my way back I discovered a few drops oosing out of the rock; and, after digging a little with the point of my bamboo and my fingers, found a small well, which was filled with water. But the water accumulated; whether impregnated with the spray of the sea, or some mineral in the rock, it was quite saltish. Withal, it was fresh when compared with the sea-water; and, after allowing the sand and mud to subside, I took a hearty draught of it; but nobody else would drink it, and I carried my four bottles home full.

On the 22d we had not a drop of fresh water with which to wet our tongues. There was no standing it any longer; so, as soon as we had eaten something in shape of breakfast, each of us tied a blanket, and four days' allowance of ghee, and rice cakes, and chickens, and a few onions, into the form of a knapsack, and, lacing it upon our backs, proceeded on our tour of discovery. Eleven of the lascars joined us; but the remaining eight stopped behind. Well knowing the propensities of these, we secreted every thing that we thought they would steal. After selecting two bottles of wine to take along with us, we stowed the only two remaining deep amongst the rice in one of the casks; the ham we buried amongst a parcel of rubbish beneath the floor of the tent; a few yams we hid beneath a large lump of turf that formed the threshold; and a handful of onions beneath a quantity of rice still a-drying. The ghee we had to leave to its fate, and the auspices of a piece of bacon stuck into it. Every thing not eatable we trusted to their mercy.

In order to prolong our stay as far as possible, we took our line and hooks along with us, and a burning rope by which we could kindle a fire. We had also provided a flag to erect, in case we should be unable to remain there, and a soda-water bottle, containing the following inscription, which we intended to suspend upon the flag-staff:—

"The Lady Munro, of Madras, was totally lost on the N.W. side of this Island, on the night of the 11th October, by which 75 souls perished. The survivors, 22 in number, are living there in the greatest misery and distress, hoping, by the grace of God, soon to find some opportunity of being rescued from their desolate abode.—20th October, 1833."

We found the ascent over the first range of mountains very steep and precipitous, rendering it necessary to keep both hands and feet in constant exertion. There was nothing to hold on by but the naked lava, and large pieces were constantly giving way, threatening those in the rear with destruction. One large fragment, in particular, tumbled over a group of lascars, and did no more damage than break a bottle of wine on one of their backs—one of the only two we had saved for the excursion. Not making due allowance for the burden upon my back, I once lost my balance, while scrambling across the brow of a rock, and fell from a considerable height; but received no injury, and profited by studying my centre of gravity better for the future. When we got to the summit of the ridge, we came to the usual jungle of reeds and rushes, higher than our heads, and as difficult to pass over (for they were too dense to be passed through) as the same depth of newly-fallen snow. Every step cost us a struggle; frequently we fell through, and reached the ground, and did not recover the top of the reeds without considerable exertion. We were obliged to halt every two hundred yards, lest we should lose some of our number; and every now and then tumbled into pits and mouths of caves, that puzzled us in getting out again. Often did we wish that some one should contain water enough to take us to the nose! About noon I was most agreeably surprised to find myself sticking amongst mud and water to the knees, and pretty nigh hard and fast. The joyful cry of "Panee mila!" (water is found) spread to the extreme end of the file, and soon brought up the rear; and, making them all sit round in a circle, I gave each a cup of water in turn.

Greatly refreshed by the water, and a piece of cake spread with ghee, and an onion, we renewed our march with increased vigour, keeping along the tops of the mountains where the jungle was light, and making very fair progress. We passed by several hills, evidently the seats of volcanoes, quite conical in appearance, and deeply convex on the top, with large masses of spongy lava strewed around, and, to appearance, not yet cooled. We had frequent showers of rain during the day. In the evening we descended into the low-lying land towards the shore; but found the jungle very heavy and fatiguing, and abounding with a kind of bushy shrub, something resembling cypress. We passed over large quantities of this brushwood, lying decayed, and bearing marks of having been burnt at some former period. There were many places where the ground had been dug up, and pieces of roots of vegetables strewed about, from which we concluded that there must be deer upon the island; but the jaw-bone we formerly found with the two canine teeth, induced us to think they might be hogs. About sunset we were so much worn out and exhausted, that we resolved to lie down amongst the reeds till morning, though only a mile from the shore. Selecting a sheltered spot in the lee of a bank, we threw down our knapsacks, rolled out a narrow bed amongst the tall reeds, and spread our supper upon our knees. But we had hardly sat down, when a fire which the lascars had kindled by means of the burning rope, communicated with the jungle, and we were instantly all in a blaze.

The thoughtless rascals, thinking they had done a fine thing, stood aloof and laughed, as the flames darted to the sky, burning up the bushes with their foliage, and crackling amongst the rubbish like musketry. We were for a few minutes undecided what to do. We thought of spreading the flames, till they should burn up a large patch, in the centre of which we might remain secure from a second conflagration; but, dreading that the strong wind, then blowing, would render the smoke and sparks insupportable, we fled off to a small naked rock to windward, and, hoping to make a stand there, set a watch, and lay down to sleep. But the fire continued to beat to windward; and about eleven our rock was surrounded, and enveloped in smoke and flames. We could have avoided the intensity of the heat, but the smoke became quite intolerable, and, abandoning our position as untenable, we burst through the circumference of flames, and fled for the shore. The light of the fire assisted us much in our retreat: we gained the bank before midnight, and, wrapping ourselves up in our blankets, slept amongst the reeds and long grass, on a precipice overlooking the sea, having taken the precaution to secure a path to the naked rocks in case of another surprise.

Being greatly fatigued, we slept till daylight without any disturbance, further than the crackling and glare of the fire. When we awoke, the flames had spread over the island for miles, and still continued to persevere to windward. Not much liking to break through the band of flame on the bank above, and become suffocated with smoke and ashes, and smouldering faggots, we attempted to lead the way along the shore; but the whole party seemed quite dispirited, and could hardly crawl from rock to rock. At last we were obliged to give in to the general wish to return to our tent, in the hope of attempting it again at a future period, when the jungle should be burned up, and the interior of the island become passable. We were now not at all sorry for the burning, and could not help remarking that our prospects were brightening. We had several times thought of setting fire to the island intentionally, as the best signal we could possibly make; but refrained from doing so, lest we should destroy the eggs and young birds, on which we might have to depend for subsistence.

About nine we had separated into two parties: one taking the route along the shore, the other over the interior of the island. Our party having fortunately discovered a pool of water, were seated around it at breakfast, when we observed the other party on the top of a hill about a mile off, waving eagerly upon us. It struck us that their number was increased; and, on counting, we found three strangers amongst them. One of these left the group, and came hurrying towards us. We all left our water, and ran to meet him; the most fatigued making as good way as the best of us, and crying out "Al-al-at!" with tears of joy flowing over their cheeks. As we neared him, we descried his low-crowned black hat, his red flannel shirt, and canvass trousers, with transport. Our only fears were lest he also should be a castaway, and as helpless as ourselves; but he seemed too comfortably rigged, and with too much of the scarlet in his complexion, to have lived long on rice and water. As we got near him, his large knife in one hand, and another smaller in his belt, convinced us what he was; and a hearty shake of his fist satisfied us of his good intentions. He told us he was a little alarmed on seeing a parcel of people whose likeness he had never seen before; he did not take them exactly for savages, but thought they might possibly be Chinese or Tartars; nor did he approach them till he had convinced himself that he had the stronger party, though not by one-half so numerous. One of the lascars could speak only a few words of English, and by "ship brook," and "plenty man drown," assisted by signs and gesticulations, convinced him that some ship had been wrecked.

We asked him a thousand questions, which he answered with patience and coolness. He told us that he belonged to an American schooner, the General Jackson, of Boston, Captain Percival; that she was lying at anchor in the lee of the island fishing, and intended sailing for the Isle of France, in a few days, to undergo repairs; that himself, and two or three more, were to remain upon the island sealing till the vessel returned; that he was then living in a cave, about two miles farther along the shore; that the fire of last night passed over his abode like a whirlwind, and almost burnt him up as he lay asleep; that he awakened perfectly confounded to account for such a phenomenon; that he at last concluded some person had mischievously set fire to the island; and that he was out to discover who had done so, when he fell in with the party. This information completed our happiness, and dispelled all our gloomy forebodings, and melancholy anticipations of the future. His name was Isaac Pierce, a native of Boston. George and Pedro were the names of the two that accompanied him, natives of the Cape de Verde islands.

After following their footsteps for half an hour along the bank, still hot and smoking, we descended over a lofty precipice, and got down to the cave on the beach; but, though called a cave, it was merely a jutting rock, that did not afford shelter from a shower. Soon after our arrival, Pierce got a kettle of fish and pork boiled for us, and, with plenty of biscuit and fine fresh water, we made the heartiest meal we had done for a fortnight.

After dinner I got a piece of a raw hogskin, and made myself a pair of brogues, such as Pierce was wearing, and found incalculable benefit from them. In the evening I went out in my new shoes upon the rocks to fish; and caught a kind of bream, four, six, and eight lbs. weight, as fast as I could take them off the hook. There was no surf here, it being the lee shore; the fish were very good to eat, and somewhat resembled ling.

On the 24th we tried to muster a party to return to our tent; but more than one-half refused, or were unable to go back. Poor Evatt was quite knocked up. After breakfast we set out with Pierce, the two Cape de Verdes, and four or five lascars, when, with constant labour and exertion, we did not get to the tent till three in the afternoon. When we arrived there, we found every thing turned upside down; our yams and ghee were nearly all consumed; our ham was gone, and the most valuable of our things carried away, and nobody knew any thing of them. The rice we intrusted to the care of those who remained was all left unturned, and become unfit for any thing; the two casks containing the dried rice were uncovered, and exposed to all weathers; but our two bottles of wine, concealed in one of them, escaped untouched.

Early on the morning of the 25th we started, with every one carrying as heavy a burden on his back as he conveniently could. Not a man remained behind. Instead of taking the direct road over the mountains, as we did formerly, we skirted along the shore, and succeeded in gaining the top of the bank, though with much difficulty and considerable danger, by scrambling along a very narrow path, skirting the brow of a precipice that overhung the sea. The path was in many places so narrow that two persons could not pass each other with safety. Knowing well that those lazy, indolent thieves, who lagged behind when we first left the tent, would be the last to leave me now, I confess that I took a malicious pleasure in heating their jackets, and trying what stuff they were made

in his movements to be dangerous, and soon sank under repeated blows of a club, which sealers carry for that purpose. Before he had time to recover from the blows, they stabbed him to the heart with a large knife, and commenced skinning him. During this operation, the female returned to the water's edge, to look for her husband, and raising her head, neck, and bosom above water, the very prototype of the mermaid, looked on in the most pitiful and imploring manner. But she, too, had almost fallen a victim to her affection; for a sturdy sealer, blind to all her tears and entreaties, gave her such a blow upon the temple as tumbled her upon her back; but she had sense and strength enough to dive, and soon disappeared. We had not proceeded fifty yards farther, when we were startled by one snorting beneath a rock on which we stood. When we looked over, we saw another pair, which, after two or three blows of the club, were also knocked down, and treated in like manner. The largest seal was about six feet long; his skin was valued at ten dollars, but the fur was the chief object. The skins are preserved by salt, and carried home, packed in casks. The lascars did not know what to make of them when they first saw them, the general opinion being that they were swine; and though they had all ate of the pork two days before, no one would go near the "soon:" after two or three conjectures, they observed their feelers or whiskers, and, concluding they must be cats, without ceremony assisted in skinning them.

About eight miles from the place where we were wrecked, on a low, stony beach, we perceived the body of a European, but too shockingly mutilated to be recognised. We saw also several pieces of our own wreck, with a beam and a piece of sponge belonging to some other that must have been thrown on shore a long time before. Near to this bay, we passed the remains of a thatched hut, that Captain P. had built about seven years before, when engaged in sealing. About two hundred yards inland, there is a deep pool of good water. This is the only place where a boat could come ashore, and take in a fresh stock without difficulty. Abundance of wood might be got a little way more inland. The fire still continued to force its way to windward, and threatened to burn up every reed on the island. The party of sealers were not at all sorry for it, for it saved them an immense deal of trouble in cutting pathways through the jungle. When we got up to the cave, only one man was found missing, a poor lascar, who had not recovered from the injuries he had received in coming on shore. Aware of his weakly condition, he set out early in the morning, expecting us to overtake him; but as we took our route along the shore, instead of over the mountains, as he expected, he was left far behind. The schooner, which we had not yet seen, had come round from the lee of the island, and was lying at anchor. What a muscle-shell she seemed! a mere wherry, and not much larger than our long-boat. For such a thing to stem the Atlantic wave, and labour round the stormy Cape, seemed impossible. Yet she had just completed a five months' cruise away among the Desolation and Crozet Islands, latitudes abounding in icebergs and continual storms, and too remote to be considered in the navigable world. Soon after we got to the cave, the captain, who had gone on to meet us, and within sight of our tent, returned. When he came to the top of the precipice, he gave a scream like a jackall, and was instantly answered by another such from the schooner, and before he got down to the beach, a boat was on shore. He was covered all over with charcoal and perspiration, so thirsty that he could hardly speak, and as hungry as a wolf. I did not much disturb him till after he had discussed a plateful of fish, and a demi-john of water; and then he was so anxious to get on board, that I could get little out of him but his resolution to be off next day. I told him how little we expected to leave the island, without having an opportunity of returning to our tent; how few things we had saved from the wreck, and that we had scarcely enough to cover our nakedness. I also mentioned the number of Royal mails, and mails of the H. E. I. C. that we had secured; but could make no impression upon him. He soon went on board, leaving me alone to bivouac with the lascars on shore. Mr. E. not being able to return to the tent the day before, remained at the cave, and was on board when we arrived; and Pierce, who had got orders to go on board immediately on his arrival, did so, and remained there all night; but I was left to the care of my kind and good Cape de Verde friends, George and Pedro, two very fine, stout, good-hearted fellows. They were of the party when we fell in with them on the morning of the fire. They could speak a few words of English, and their first question when I met them was, whether I could speak English? and when I convinced them that I could, they relieved me of my knapsack, asked if I was hungry, and told me I would soon come to their house, and get plenty of fish,—shaking their heads, and ejaculating every minute, "D——d sight!"

After two days' acquaintance I found them kinder than ever; and when the captain went on board, they did every thing they could to please me. I was very thirsty, and asked for a draught of water; but all the water was expended, and the spring a good way off: nevertheless, Pedro, though he had travelled over from the tent the same day, and must have been much fatigued and hungry, threw the little water-cask over his shoulder, went away, and returned with it full, about half an hour after. Meantime, George had kindled a fire, and made me a jug of chocolate as soon as the water arrived. They then cleared a berth for me to sleep on, picked up all the largest stones, made it as smooth as they could, and, spreading my blanket over it, placed a bundle of clothes for my pillow; and, leaving the water-cask beside me lest I should become thirsty before morning, bade me good night, and lay down at a little distance from me, repeating their favourite phrase, "D——d sight!" with particular energy. I was asleep in a few minutes after, and never once awoke till daylight. I arose quite as refreshed as if I had slept on a bed of roses,

"Under a canopy of costly state,
And lulled with sounds of sweetest melody."

Early on the morning of the 26th, a boat came off from the schooner, with the message that every one who wished to leave the island must go on board without delay, as she was about getting under weigh. As soon as I got on board, I again represented to the captain our condition, and requested him to allow us an opportunity of returning to our tent for another burden of clothes, and other necessaries, which the coldness of the season, and our situation, so much required; and which we could have done in a day and a half, or even in one day, if he would send a boat as far along the shore as he could have done, with safety from the surf, to pick us up on our return in the evening; but all was to no purpose: he was determined to be off—and off he did go, about ten o'clock, leaving a boat and six of the most efficient of his crew upon the island. The convict Forsyth hid himself when we were embarking, and escaped. The poor lascar whom we left behind on the journey of the previous day, not coming forward in time, was also left upon the island. I would readily sympathise with his condition,—a poor, weakly

Bengalee, left in bondage from the severity of his wound, and separated from his stronger and more fortunate companions; with all the inveterate prejudices and antipathies of caste; with habits diametrically opposite to the Americans; so much so, that he would consider their touching his food a poison and an abomination; and, withal, unable to explain a thought, or to speak or understand a word of any language intelligible to either; with the prospects of home and dear relations brightening on his view, cast again into the impenetrable gloom of doubt and despair, and no one now to share in his affliction, or to listen to his tale. I had a great desire to take one of the ship's dogs with me—one that was wont to lie at my feet at night, and follow me wherever I went, even over precipices where I thought she could not possibly follow; but some one, with barbarous dishonesty, had conveyed her out of the way. When the anchor was weighed, I saw the poor thing running about the place where I went into the boat, in the most anxious manner, as if she would have plunged into the water to get after me. Before sunset, Amsterdam was sunk beneath the wave.

We were a good deal vexed to go away so destitute, and leave so many things behind us, which had cost us so much trouble to collect. Many of these were of intrinsic value, such as several pieces of plate, jewels, &c., and many others possessed an imaginary value, appreciated by the relations of the deceased. We had collected one or two relics of almost every passenger on board, with the intention of sending them to their relations; and these, instead of becoming sacred in the estimation of a parent or a friend, and of being cherished in lasting remembrance of those that were dear to them, must now be torn to pieces by avaricious hands, doled out in payment for the necessaries of life, or hawked about for sale at the command of any wretch who can only advance the dollars.

Yes! that richly-carved tortoise-shell comb, that checked the luxuriant flow of the auburn tresses of ——, may be stuck into the matted, greasy locks of some fishmonger's daughter! That Persian blade may nerve the hand of some midnight murderer, or avenge the insult of some brothel inmate! That Leghorn and that parasol may be expanded to hide the shame of some houseless, hopeless protegee, about to plunge into the dissipation of the world! These bracelets and earrings may figure in a saloon, upon some cast-off milliner's apprentice; and that unfinished blue-black silken gown may be worn out, and patched, and bespattered by the vilest on the earth, and cut up into baby-clouts by the guilty mother of some bastard brat! Fine pickings the Americans will no doubt have of it! The Cape de Verde natives can dive like seals, and will pick up every silver spoon, every piece of coin, of which there was a great deal on board; and the *General* will go home with his pockets loaded with as many copper bolts, anchors, and chain cables, coir hawsers, coils of ropes, and bolts of canvass, as will keep him in tear and wear for the rest of his days.

But what is to become of all these boxes of Royal and Hon. East India Company's Mails and Post Office Packets, in which the Indian community undoubtedly have so much at stake? Surely something will be done by the Government at the Isle of France to rescue them from rapacious hands, and either to restore them to their original owners, or forward them to their destination. As nearly as I can recollect, there were six boxes, some of them at least a foot in length, and of proportionate breadth and thickness. Some of them were broken open, but several were still entire, under their wax-cloth covers. Besides these, there were several parcels in wax-cloth, belonging to private persons, amongst the addresses of which I remember Mr. Ball, and Mr. B. M., Van Diemen's Land. There was also a number of detached letters to private individuals. We had taken considerable pains in collecting them all together, and had them safely lodged in our tent.

CHAPTER IV.

"Once more upon the waters! Yet once more!
And the waves bound beneath me, as a steed
That knows his rider. Welcome to their roar!
Swift be their guidance, wheresoe'er it lead;
Though the strained mast should quiver as a reed,
And the rent canvass fluttering strew the gale,
Still must I on; for I am as a weed,
Flung from the rock on ocean's foam, to sail
Where'er the surge may sweep, the tempest's breath prevail."

On the morning of the 27th of October, we were once more upon the wide ocean, mounting over the waves, in as tight a little craft as could swim, with her three-bonneted sails spread out to the breeze, and ploughing up the brine to the depth of five feet and a half. We expected to arrive at the Mauritius in twelve or fourteen days; but we had water enough to last us twenty-six days, and plenty of rice, and pork, and fish, for all on board. The wind was pretty fair, and the weather pro-

F 3

mised to be good. I was busy all day washing my clothes; clearing away the smoke, and charcoal, and perspiration, from my face, hands, and feet; repairing my pantaloons; paring my ragged nails; combing my long uncombed hair; shaving my overgrown beard; detaching the loose skin from my hands and feet; and treating my sores and bruises, grown callous by constant irritation. The lascars were also busy making themselves more comfortable; cutting up gowns and pelisses, and tucking them together for their own wearing, and sheathing themselves in flannel.

Our crew consisted of the captain, his mate, and two blacks. The gross weight of our cargo, and dead weight on board, was ten or twelve tons; yet she was as stiff as a salmon coble, and as tight as a cask; and, though every little babbling wave washed her decks, we were as dry below as a pepper-box. The captain spoke of the *General's* power, as a sea-boat, in the highest terms; and the confusion he had frequently occasioned to large ships, by overhauling them in spite of all their exertions to keep such a piratical-looking craft at a respectable distance, when it required the display of all the stripes and stars he could hoist, to restore them to composure. He said that in heavy weather she did not wait to go over the waves, but bored her nose straight through, and came out at the other side. She appeared to justify the high opinion of the captain; and, so far as personal safety was concerned, I could have gone round the world in her as willingly as on board any Indiaman; and would ever keep in mind this advantage, that where the *General* could get on shore, I would have many chances in my favour of getting high and dry also.

Captain P. was a regular veteran to his trade, and had been knocking about in these high southern latitudes, all round the world, since 1799, to the great destruction of seals, and whales, and sea-elephants. Happening, when in London several years ago, to hear of an island being discovered to the southward of New Zealand, he hurried home to America; and, hoping to reap the first fruits, cleared out for the reported island with all despatch. About four months after, he made the latitude and longitude given out; but, after cruising about in all directions near it, he was forced to give up the pursuit as hopeless. He had lately been away amongst the Falkland, the Crozet, and Desolation Islands; but met with nothing except icebergs and snow showers, and incessant storms, sufficient to blow the few remaining "hairs off his head." Finding the surf in all places so high as to render it perilous to land a boat, he gave up the pursuit of the elephants; and, at the expense of having the head of his foremast carried away, his larboard bulwark stove in, and the prospect of foundering every minute, stood down for his old and nearly-forgotten friend Amsterdam. He made the island during the night of the 16th of October; and, passing within a few miles of our tent, went round, and came to anchor on the lee side. He had lived for three years at a time upon the island, sealing; and knew every creek, and bluff-head, and cave, by name. In 1799, he introduced a breed of hogs; these had increased and multiplied a thousand fold, and formed the chief subsistence of his party. I tasted one that they had shot two days before we embarked, and liked it much better than domestic pork. They live upon the roots of reeds and plants, and are very dexterous in plundering the eggs of the sea-birds, and capturing the young ones, and even the old ones themselves, if they can get at them. On that account very few birds build their nests on places accessible to them. In days prior to the *swine democracy*, the ground was literally covered with eggs at certain seasons. Several years ago he shipped a living cargo of them for the Mauritius; but there being a deficiency in his commissariat, he sacrificed the weaker to gratify the cravings of the stronger, and saved the hog-fed majority to bring a good price in Port Louis. During our abode upon the island we never saw a hog, though we often saw their traces. Captain P. was more fortunate; for he had not walked a mile, when two half-grown ones crossed his path at full squeak and cantering, and singed all over. About seven years before this, he landed a breed of goats and dunghill fowls. All the goats are now dead except two large males, which are as wild as deer. A few of the fowls still survive; but they are no less wild than their bearded contemporaries.

A great number of penguins and albatrosses

hatch on the island; their eggs may be procured in abundance during nine months of the year,—they are very good eating. According to Captain P., a young albatross is as tender as a chicken, and as great a dainty as a young turkey; however, it was not our fortune to fall in with any of these delicacies.

I could fancy the climate of Amsterdam pleasant enough; but the soil seems unlikely to repay any degree of cultivation, the surface being chiefly covered with loose fragments of lava, strewed over in certain places with a few handfuls of soil—but the greater part is covered with a soft, spongy kind of turf. Captain P. spoke of the contiguous island (St. Paul's) in much more favourable terms. It is much less mountainous, and contains a considerable deal of good soil. It is also colonized with hogs, and contains a variety of garden vegetables, growing wild. It is remarkable for a fine large basin or harbour, about two miles and a half in circumference, where one hundred sail of the line might lie at anchor, in 29 fathoms water, in safety from all winds. The entrance to the basin is not more than 30 yards wide, and it does not contain more than six feet water; however, as the bottom is covered with loose stones, they could easily be removed, so as to allow of large ships entering it in safety. A strong current runs in and out with the rise and fall of the tide, rendering it dangerous to enter, unless with the flowing tide. The basin has been discovered to be the remains of a volcanic crater.

Near to the basin there are some very hot mineral springs, which deposit a large quantity of sulphur when allowed to subside. A thermometer rises in them to 212°, so as to admit of fish being boiled in them. Some of these springs are so near the basin, that fishes may be thrown off the hook, out of their native element, and boiled in them. Captain P. has frequently made salt, by filling a boiler with sea-water, and set it afloat in one of them to boil, till the salt crystallized.

So long as Britain retains possession of such a rendezvous for shipping as Port Louis, this harbour would be of little importance; but if ever the flourishing colonies of Australia or Tasmania become independent, this barren, neglected island will be the keystone of their empires, and be converted into one of the safest and most commodious harbours in the world. In the meantime, these two islands are only frequented once in a number of years by a solitary party of sealers, or by a chance ship heaving-to, to take a boatful of fresh fish. They are about fifty miles distant from one another, and nearly in the same meridian. Captain P. did not think any person had been upon the island of Amsterdam for the last seven years. On that account he anticipated a rich harvest of seal-skins—perhaps 2000, amounting in value to nearly £4000.

There is a great deal of confusion about the names of these islands. In all English charts, the northern of the two is called Amsterdam, and the southern St. Paul's; but, according to American authority, their names are inversed. They were discovered by the Dutch navigator Vlaming, in 1697, and named by him as they are done in English charts. According to Horsburgh, the circumference of Amsterdam is only twelve miles; but Captain P., who had travelled round and round it for years, said it was not less than thirty, which agrees with my own experience.

On the 30th October, the lascars were all very busily employed cutting up webs and clothes, and sewing them again, according to their own fashion. We expressed a strong desire to have their bags examined, to claim those things which were our own, and only those things which bore the evidence of our written name; but Capt. P. took a different view of the case, and postponed it till we should get to the Isle of France, promising that every thing should be done most honourably, according to our desire. I could that morning boast of a clean, I mean a newly-washed shirt, the first I had on for a long time; I felt it quite a luxury, and so I might, for it took me half of the previous day to wash it. It was rather a favourite, being the only one originally my own, and still, with all my treading, and beating, and dragging in the wake, it was not so white as it might have been, and yet the salt water was clear enough.

On the 4th of the succeeding month, in the afternoon, we sighted a small vessel, and thinking her bound to New South Wales, I wrote out a short report of the shipwreck, and boarded her. She turned out to be the Eagle of Hobart Town, Capt. Pratt, bound from Port Louis to Sydney. The captain was very kind indeed to us; offered, in the most liberal manner, to do any thing for us in his power; and learning that the *General* was very low in spirits, (there being nothing in shape of grog on board,) obliged us to accept of a dozen of port wine. He had experienced bad weather for some time, which had carried away one of his top-masts, and sprung a leak, which obliged him to pump every half hour, but he did not think it dangerous.

Captain P. told us on the 10th that several of the lascars had been trying to come to terms with his second mate, wishing him to take all their valuables into his care, and keep them till they could find a convenient opportunity of getting them back again, when they got on shore at Port Louis. The captain seemed quite indignant at the proposal, and said he enjoined his mate, in the strictest manner, to have no dealings whatever with the lascars. We again represented to him our desire to have a search immediately, and tried to convince him of the inconveniences of delaying to do so till we got into a harbour crowded with shipping; but he assured us that every one should be carefully examined, and if he suspected any connivance in his own crew, he would cause every corner and locker in the schooner to be examined.

If I did not know then what a state of widowhood was, then I never could know. I rued that I was a bachelor-widower, but that was nothing to the purpose. There was I, with scarcely an object of past enjoyment to look upon, or to recall one pleasing association. All the partners of my cares and of my pleasures—all the resources of my idle and gloomy hours—and all the sharers of my fortune, were swept away. The first-born fruits of my pen and my pencil, and the unfledged thoughts of later years, were all gone, and I had none left on which to dote with a father's eye—to nurture with paternal care, or to train up to hardy, healthy maturity.

Where was my desk, with my most secret thoughts intrusted to its hinges? Where was my journal? Where were my tokens of remembrance? Where was my portfolio? Where was anything formerly my own? Yes! there is the ring upon my finger,—that is something; but there is also the hair upon my head, and the nails upon my fingers. But for these I have not the waves to thank; no, nor for the soul within my body. It was through no lenity or forbearance in them that this, its earthly tabernacle, was not bleaching upon the shelves of Amsterdam. Why, though I had died and been born again, I could not have found myself more destitute, or more unconnected with tangible material.

We began to look out for land on the 11th, and having no chronometer, but depending upon the dead reckoning alone, we were resolved to err upon the safe side. All my fears, and all my dread of approaching land in darkness, again sprung to life, and kept me in a state of nervous irritability. My ear was as sensible to the slightest noise, as if it had been the bump of a ship upon the rocks.

> ——————————"Oh, gentle sleep!
> Nature's soft nurse, how have I frightened thee,
> That thou no more wilt weigh my eyelids down,
> And steep my senses in forgetfulness!"

Every trimming of the sails, every lurch, every wave that broke on board, made me start from my sleep, and next moment I found myself on deck. It was to no purpose that I reflected upon its folly, and tried to reason myself into coolness and self-possession. I had no sooner crept into my berth, and wooed and won a sort of dreamy oblivion, than something or another broke the charm, and again I was on deck.

On the 13th we made the Round Island, to the northward of the Mauritius, about noon, and rounded the Gunner's Queen an hour after dark, when we stood along the shore, within hearing of the surf, towards Port Louis. But our little craft, with more than her usual cleverness, outshot the reckoning so far, that, when daylight appeared, we had passed the harbour many miles, and were opposite the south-west point of the island. Strange to say, there is no light-house at Port Louis. We then tacked about, and continued to beat to windward, till noon on the 14th, before we made the anchorage. About two miles from Port Louis, we saw the hull of a large ship, the "Cæsar," lying on the shore, and could not help envying the condition of the passengers, compared to that of ours. What a comfortable shipwreck they must have had, with no other inconvenience than just to pack up their baggage, and convey it ashore at their leisure—walk to a comfortable inn, and sit down at their ease, and laugh over their good fortune!

When we let go our anchor at the bell buoy, waiting till the health officer should come alongside, every eye was upon us, and telescopes were levelled against us from every ship within sight. Seeing the deck crowded with people, some thought we were a parcel of pirates, driven in by distress, —some took us for a slaver, that had lost her reckoning, and run unconsciously into the hands of justice; whilst others, nearer the mark, took us for the crew of some ship cast away, who had built our vessel out of the wreck, and got once more within sight of an inhabited land.

About two hours after we came to anchor, the surgeon's boat, with his yellow flag, stood down the harbour, and he came on board. There being neither plague nor cholera prevalent amongst the inhabitants of Amsterdam, we were beyond the pale of quarantine, and were allowed to land.

CHAPTER V.

As soon as the news of our arrival was known, I had a warm invitation from Messrs. Jack and Henderson, with whom I had formed a casual acquaintance, when the Lady Munro called at Port Louis, to go and live with them; and the captain, showing no regard to his promise respecting the searching of the lascars, I went on shore in the afternoon, and had the house, the wardrobe, and the purse of these kind gentlemen at my disposal.

Next morning I had a visit from several of the lascars, decked off in flowing robes, the originals of which were painfully remembered. They were all living under the protection, and at the expense of Government, in houses appropriated for their use. They gave me a long account of their goings on, and amused me a good deal. The Burra-tindel informed me, that the mate of the schooner, (Mr. Fuller,) seeing a part of the police coming off, told them that, if they had any valuables, they had better intrust him with them, and he would keep them till they found it convenient to take them ashore; that unless they did so, everything would be taken from them by the police. The Burra-tindel told me he gave over his things, consisting of fifteen silver spoons, of different sizes; a silver watch, and a silver cup. Musdeer, one of the lascars, gave also a silver cup; and several others gave more or less. After they had been examined by the police, they went to the mate, and asked him for those things they delivered to his charge; but all the answer he gave them was, some person had stolen them from him, and what could he do? Of course, the captain knew nothing about it. But all were not so easily imposed upon. Sammy, one of the cuddy servants, contrived to smuggle ashore six large silver spoons, and four silver forks; but they were all stolen from him next day by some of the rest. Munoo, one of the tindels, the most mutinous man of the crew, had bills of exchange upon him to the amount of £2,300: these were taken into custody by the police, besides a quantity of plate from several others. But Salmin, an old African, not worth a rupee to look at, and who drew from the skipper the remark, that "God Almighty showed no partiality for fine forms and features, when he saved him from the wreck," was proof against both the insinuations of the mate, and the searching of the police, and contrived to save no less than fifty-six sovereigns. The plan he took was rather ingenious. Finding an old-fashioned sword-belt amongst the wreck, composed of two folds of leather sewed together, he cut open one of the seams, and, stowing away his gold, sewed it up again, and wore it as a belt for an old knife which he attached to it. He was now playing the liberal with great profusion; treating his companions to beef, and fish, and curry, and fruit, to excess; lending any one a handful of rupees that wanted it; and making every one that was thirsty as drunk as himself. I always believed that, if any one of the lascars had anything valuable, Salmin was the one; for, though the most useless creature to look at of all, he was always on the search morning and evening; and I had frequently found him sitting behind a rock, all alone, with a bottle of wine in his hand, and with the neck broken off. Withal, he was less selfish than any man amongst them. Our cellar was indebted to him for three or four bottles. He once told us of his having discovered a quantity of yams, and a small supply of water, in a cask that had been overlooked, and occasionally brought us a few cakes and birds to eat. He was one of the mizzen-top boys on board, and contributed a good deal to our amusement there. He was never a minute idle, and did his work well. He was wont to hint, that it would be a profitable speculation for some one to buy him; and when asked his terms, divided the concern into two lots—himself and his cap; but placed a sufficient value upon the latter to make up for the money he had on his person. He was to have given up all intentions of ever going to sea again, and to enter into my service in

Bengal as a chowkedan; but I embarked in too great a hurry to conclude the agreement.

Next morning, the 21st, I learned that a ship (the Caroline) had touched at the island, and was to put to sea again next day for Calcutta. I lost no time in calling on her agents, Messrs. Pearson and Chapman, and accepted the terms they proposed for a passage. I offered to give them a bill for the amount on any agent in Calcutta; or, if they preferred it, an order on the Presidency Paymaster, to draw it in monthly instalments of Sic. R. 100; but neither of these terms would they accept of, though they knew my situation perfectly, and that I was a total stranger in Port Louis; yet nothing but the "cash advance" would satisfy them. I felt very much hurt by the interview, the issue of which I so little expected, and had my irritable feelings probed to the quick by the unfeeling thrust of self-interest. I felt for the first time the poverty of my situation, and that my credit was then not worth a dollar, and that an Englishman could behave with as little generosity as a Hottentot, or a Laplander, or a bazaar Hindoo.

Anxious to put an end to my state of widowhood and destitution, and to return to India as speedily as possible, I immediately after wrote a statement of my case to Government, and requested the loan of as much money as would pay my expenses on the island, and my passage to India. I called upon the Secretary next forenoon to learn the result of my proposal, and to my great satisfaction had as much money as I required (£80 sterling) most liberally offered me. By mere accident, I heard that the Caroline, instead of sailing in the morning as was intended, had postponed it till the evening. I had then three hours to prepare for embarkation. I went to the Treasury and got my money, paid down my passage, and was on board before sunset.

I mention this, not with the intention of holding the mirror up to Mr. P., with whom I had to deal; for his optic lens is too suffused with the phantasmagoria of sous and marquees to profit by the picture, and his focal distance too contracted by the circumvallations of self-interest to consider anything beyond. My object is to save the feelings of any sick brother officer, who, in the pursuit of health like myself, may happen to meet with a similar misfortune; and when the loss of the last piece of clothing on his back, and every rupee he had in the world, forces him, though still convalescent, to return to his Presidency, he may have his intentions frustrated, his feelings mortified, and the most honourable terms a destitute stranger has in his power to offer coolly rejected, with the niggardly profit-and-loss calculation of a narrow-minded creature of halfpence and farthings.

On the morning of the 23d, the naked peaks of the Mauritius loomed on the horizon. I left the island with strong impressions in favour of its climate, and wondered that it was so little frequented by Indian invalids. To be sure, it has the character of being a very expensive place, but, with a little provident care, it might be a good deal mitigated. It would not do well for a subaltern, depending upon his bare pay, to take up his abode at one of the two hotels, and exert his economy to live on less than 20 or 30 rupees a-day; neither would it be advisable for him to delay refitting his wardrobe, till he could do it here at some two or three hundred per cent. higher than he could do it in India. From inquiries at good authority, I found that a snug little house, what is called a "Twelve dozen chest," can be got, in a respectable part of the town, for Sic. R. 40 a-month, and in the country for less. The establishment of servants requisite is only two, and these can readily be got here for Sic. R. 16 per month each. The table expenses might be got for about Sic. R. 40, and wines and liqueurs are moderate enough. An officer going there on sick leave should take all the furniture he is likely to require, as also everything except the mere necessaries of life, and the produce of the island. By taking these precautions, he may live almost as reasonably as he could do with his regiment. A horse or a buggy is not much required here, where every one walks on foot, and at all hours of the day. If he should become tired of the island, he can find a passage almost every week, either to the Cape or Van Diemen's Land, for about £40.

The island is most romantic, abounding in picturesque scenery, where the waterfalls, the forest, the cane-covered valley, and the steep, craggy, mist-shrouded mountain, mingle in happiest combination. Its shores are fringed with the tamarind, the cocoa, and the palmyra; studded with the most beautiful shells, reefed with tree-like coral, of all the hues of the rainbow, and washed with an ocean "darkly, deeply, beautifully blue."

The temperature is most congenial, constantly ventilated by the bracing S.E. trade, and varied by the sunshine and the shower; perhaps a little too hot out of doors, during the summer season in the lowlands, but admitting of easy transitions to higher regions, where a cooler atmosphere may be enjoyed. All the inhabitants speak in high terms of the climate, and their very healthy appearance does not contradict them.

A smattering of French is very useful to a stranger on arriving here; it is the popular language,—even the slaves have adopted it. It is also the language of the Court and the Press. The Botanical Gardens, about ten miles from Port Louis, form a most interesting lounge: there one may wander alone, through long alleys of the rarest trees, impervious to the solar ray, accompanied by little streamlets of crystal water, rippling over the shining pebbles that seem to float upon the surface, in convoy with the newly-fallen unfaded flowers of purple, and carnation, and golden hue; or recline upon a carpet of closely-cropped grass, embroidered with miniature flowers, with the luxuriant branches of an infinite variety of palm trees waving over head; or botanize amidst the images of the most various plants and shrubs, on the banks of an island also, rendered now and then conspicuous and wonderful by the sparkling [illegible] of a variegated fleet of feathered insects, or sequester himself in forest solitude and silence, broken only by the breath of the softest breeze, or the rustling of the insect wing, and inhale the ambrosial perfumes of odoriferous leaves,

"[illegible]"

till he could fancy himself transplanted into the Garden of Eden.

FINIS.

GLASGOW:
PRINTED BY W. [illegible], FREE PRESS OFFICE.

CPSIA information can be obtained at www.ICGtesting.com
Printed in the USA
BVOW07s1822090514

353095BV00008B/222/P